A to Z of English Ter

Learn Verb Tense in 2 Days

By Bandana Ojha

Introduction

Effective communication skills are necessary for all students and people of all professions and effective communication is achieved by the concept of English verb tenses. There are three tenses, past tenses, present tense and the future and four sub- categories of three tenses like simple, progressive, perfect and perfect progressive. It is important to understand well how to use these tenses with the forms of verbs. Everyone should know how to conjugate verbs properly by focusing on the structures of tenses and modal tenses, so that they can create clear and effective sentences.

This book will help everyone to learn verb tense just in two days with clear under standings, guideline and explanations of all three tenses present, past and future and their division, simple, progressive, perfect and perfect progressive. with hundreds of real like examples. The book will make sure you speak, write and understand English with confidence.

A to Z of English Tense is excellent book for all who wants to learn English Tense in two days.

Please check this out:

Our other best-selling books for kids are-

My First Fruits

Most Popular Animal Quiz book for Kids: 100 amazing animal facts

Quiz Book for Kids: Science, History, Geography, Biology, Computer & Information Technology

English Grammar for Kids: Most Easy Way to learn English Grammar

Solar System & Space Science- Quiz for Kids: What You Know About Solar System

Know about Sharks: 100 Amazing Fun Facts with Pictures

Know About Whales:100+ Amazing & Interesting Fun Facts with Pictures: " Never known Before "- Whales facts

Know About Dinosaurs: 100 Amazing & Interesting Fun Facts with Pictures

Know About Kangaroos: Amazing & Interesting Facts with Pictures

Know About Penguins: 100+ Amazing Penguin Facts with Pictures

Know About Dolphins :100 Amazing Dolphin Facts with Pictures

100 Amazing Quiz Q & A About Penguin: Never Known Before Penguin Facts

English Grammar Practice Book for elementary kids: 1000+ Practice Questions with Answers

A to Z of English Tense

All About New York: 100+ Amazing Facts with Pictures

All About New Jersey: 100+ Amazing Facts with Pictures

All About California: 100+ Amazing Facts with Pictures

All About Arizona: 100+ Amazing Facts with Pictures

All About Massachusetts: 100+ Amazing Facts with Pictures

All About Italy: 100+ Amazing Facts with Pictures

Tense

What is Tense

-Tense is the form of a verb that takes to show the time it happened.

-It is an inflectional form of a verb expressing a specific time distinction.

-Tense of a verb tells you when a person did something or when something existed or happened.

Different Types of Tenses

Time which denotes now is present, Time which denotes ago or before is past. and time denotes after or later is future.

There are three main tenses:

Present tense: Things that are true when the words are spoken or written.

For Example: John plays football every day. In this sentence, plays shows that it is a present tense

Past tense: Things that were true before the words were spoken or written.

For Example: John went to school. In this sentence, went shows that it is a past tense.

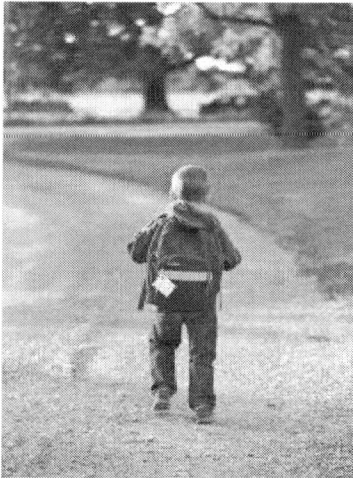

Future tense: Things that will be true after the words are spoken or written.

For Example: Student will go back home after school. In this sentence, will shows that it is a future tense.

Sub-Division of tense

Each of present, past and future tense is subdivided into four groups.

(a) Simple (Indefinite)

(b) Progressive (Continuous)

(c) Perfect

(d) Perfect Progressive(Perfect Continuous)

Sub-Division of tense

Simple	Progressive	Perfect	Perfect Progressive
Present-Simple	Present-Progressive	Present-Perfect	Present- Perfect Progressive

Past-Simple	Past-Progressive	Past-Perfect	Past- Perfect Progressive
Future-Simple	Future-Progressive	Future-Perfect	Future- Perfect Progressive

Present Tense

As described above there are four types of present Tense

1. Present Simple or Present Indefinite

2. Present Progressive or Present Continuous

3. Present Perfect

4. Present Perfect Progressive or Present Perfect Continuous

Present Simple Tense

It is also named as Present Indefinite Tense. The simple present is the most commonly used verb form in English. Over 50% of verbs in English are in the simple present tense. It's an important tense and easy to learn.

Examples of the simple present tense

Here are some example sentences showing different ways that we can use the simple present tense:

To state facts:

The sun rises in the east.

More Examples:

The earth moves around the sun.

Birds have wings.

The President of USA lives in the White House.

A dog has four legs.

London is a large city.

Water freezes at zero degrees

To describe habits and routines:

I brush my teeth every day.

I wake up at 7:00.

He drinks tea at breakfast.

The children to school by school bus.

She only eats Pizza.

I do exercises regularly.

He always studies hard for exams.

To describe feelings and opinions:

You are happy.

The child needs its mother.

I love cake.

I smell cookies.

Sarah loves toys.

How to form "Present Simple" Sentence

In simple present, most regular verbs use the root form, except in the third-person singular which ends in "s".

For a few verbs, the third-person singular ends with -es instead of -s. Typically, these are verbs whose root form ends in o, ch, sh, th, ss, gh, or z.

This is the structure to form a present simple or present indefinite sentence.

Subject+ Verb+ Rest of the Sentence

Subject	Verb	rest of sentence
I	go	to park every sunday.
We	like	to eat ice-cream.
You	write	good stories.
He/She/Jack	sleeps	at 9 pm.
They	live	in New York.

Note:

Person	Singular	Plural
1st person	I	We
2nd person	You	You
3rd person	He, She, It	They

How to form Simple Present "negative sentence"

When creating negative sentences, we usually use the auxiliary verbs do not and does not + the base form of the verb. You can also use the contraction don't or doesn't instead of do not or does not.

This is the structure to form a present simple negative sentence.

Subject+ do not/ does not + verb+ rest of the Sentence

Subject	Aux. verb (do/does) + not	Verb	Rest of sentence
I	don't	like	pizza.
We	don't	play	guitars.
You	don't	drink	milk every day.

He	doesn't	pass	the exam.
They	don't	live	in London.

Note:

Do not is used for both 1st and 2nd person singular and plural

Does not is used for 3rd person singular.

How to form Simple Present "Interrogative sentence"

To create a question that will be answered with a yes or no, start the question with Do or Does, then add a subject (the person or thing that does the action) followed by the base form of the verb and only then add the rest of the sentence.

This is the structure to form a present simple Interrogative sentence.

Auxiliary Verb (Do/Does) + Subject+ Verb+ Rest of the Sentence?

Axillary verb	Subject	Verb	rest of sentence
Do	I	ask	you

			something?
Do	you	need	any help?
Does	he	watch	cartoon movies?
Do	they	live	in New York?

How to form Simple Present "Interrogative negative sentence"

This is the structure to form a present simple Interrogative negative sentence.

Auxiliary Verb (Do/Does) + Subject+ not+ Verb+ Rest of the Sentence?

Aux. verb	Subject	not	Verb	rest of sentence
Do	I	not	play	baseball?
Do	you	not	eat	pizza?
Does	he	not	watch	TV?
Do	they	not	live	in London?

Present- Progressive

It is also named as Present Continuous. The present progressive tense is used for an on-going action in the present. Approximately 5% of verbs in spoken English are in the present continuous form.

The present continuous is used in several instances:

To describe something which is happening at the exact moment of speech:

The boy is eating a strawberry.

To describe an action that is taking place now but not at the exact moment of speech:

My father is working in Chicago.

To describe an event planned in the future:

My father is leaving for New York this evening.

It is often used for descriptions:

This little girl is wearing a beautiful dress.

To describe an action that is taking place now and is subject to interruption:

Jack cannot come to play since he is sleeping.

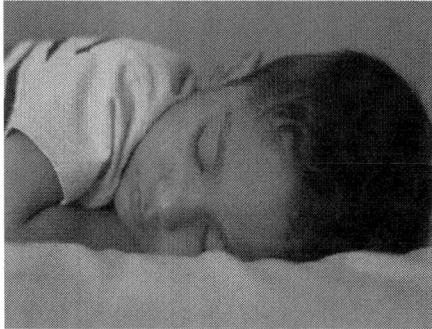

How to form "Present Progressive" Sentence

The present progressive (continuous) is formed using am, is or are together with the ing (present participle) form of the verb.

This is the structure to form a present progressive sentence.

Subject +auxiliary verb (am/is/are) + main verb (present participle)+ Rest of the Sentence

Subject	Aux. verb	Main Verb (Present Participle/ing form)	Rest of sentence
I	am	walking	in the lawn.
We	are	moving	to our new house next week.
You	are	eating	your meal.
She	is	sleeping	right now.
They	are	coming	to play with us.

How to form Present Progressive "negative sentence"

The negative in the present progressive tense is created using am not, is not or are not together with the ing form (present participle) of the verb.

This is the structure to form a present progressive negative sentence.

Subject +auxiliary verb (am/is/are) + not + main verb (present participle)+ Rest of the Sentence

Note :

When shortening a form of be and negative, just remove the o in not and add an apostrophe (')

is not > isn't

are not > aren't

Subject	auxiliary verb	not	Main Verb (Present Participle/ing form)	Rest of sentence
I	am	not	learning	new skills.
We	are	not	playing	together.

You	are	not	eating	healthy food.
She	is	not	studying	her books.
They	are	not	coming	to play with us.

How to form Present Progressive "Question sentence"

This is the structure to form a present progressive Interrogative sentence.

Auxiliary Verb (is/am/are) + Subject + main verb (present participle) + rest of the sentence?

Aux. verb	Subject	Verb	Rest of sentence
Am	I	talking	too much?
Are	we	buying	Pizza for lunch?
Are	you	playing	Football?
Is	he	watching	TV?
Are	they	laughing	at me.

How to form Present Progressive "Interrogative negative sentence"

This is the structure to form a present progressive Interrogative negative sentence.

Auxiliary Verb (is/as/are) + Subject+ not+ main verb (present participle) + rest of the sentence?

Aux. verb	Subject	not	Verb	rest of sentence
Am	I	not	reading	my books?
Are	you	not	listening	to me?
Is	he	not	watching	TV?
Are	they	not	coming	with us?

Present- Perfect

The present perfect is a grammatical combination of the present tense and perfect aspect that is used to express a past event that has present consequences. It is used to indicate a link between the present and the past.

There are many different situations where the present perfect tense can be used. It can be used in the following ways:

To describe an action that is being repeated between the past and present.

We have gone to Disneyland many times.

To describe an action that started in the past and is continuing in the present.

We have lived in New York since 2000.

To describe an action that has not yet been finished.

It has rained a lot this year.

To describe an action that was completed in the recent past.

I have just finished my lunch quickly.

To describe an action when time was not an important aspect.

Someone has eaten my pizza!

How to form "Present Perfect" Sentence

In order to form a sentence in the present perfect, choose a subject the person or thing that has done the action, add an auxiliary (or helping) verb: has or have + the past participle form of the verb and then add the rest of the sentence.

Subject+ aux. verb(have/has) + main verb (past participle) + rest of the sentence

Subject	have/has +Verb(V3) Past participle	Rest of sentence
I	have played	basketball.
We	have waited	for the train.

You	have met	him before.
Jack	has kept	my books.
He	has lived	here for 5 years.
They	have eaten	their lunch.

How to form Present Perfect "negative sentence"

When creating negative sentences, we usually use hasn't or haven't together + the V3 (past participle) form of the verb. Save the long forms (has not and have not) for when you want to create emphasis. When speaking, put the stress on 'not'.

Subject+ aux. verb(have/has) + not + main verb (past participle) + rest of the sentence

Subject	auxiliary verb	not	Verb(V3) Past participle	Rest of sentence

I	have	not	played	basketball.
We	have	not	gone	to Paris.
You	have	not	met	me before.
He	has	not	kept	my books.
Jack	has	not	lived	here.
They	have	not	eaten	their lunch.

How to form Present perfect "Interrogative sentence"

Auxiliary Verb (has/have) + Subject+ Verb(v3)+ Rest of the Sentence?

Axillary verb	Subject	Verb (past participle)	rest of sentence
Have	I	ridden	your bike?
Have	you	written	good stories?
Has	he	watched	TV?
Have	they	lived	in New York?

How to form Present perfect negative "Interrogative sentence"

Auxiliary Verb (has/have) + Subject +not+ Verb(v3)+ Rest of the Sentence?

Aux. verb	Subject	not	Verb	rest of sentence
Have	I	not	gone	there?
Have	you	not	eaten	pizza?
Has	he	not	watched	TV?
Have	they	not	lived	here?

Present- Perfect Progressive

The present perfect progressive (continuous) is used to describe an event that started in the past but is still happening in the present. That event in the present can be a habitual event or something that is taking place at this moment.

There are situations where the present perfect progressive tense can be used.

Actions that started in the past and continue in the present:

The sirens have been blaring for hours.

Actions that started in the past but just recently stopped:

Jim has been sleeping all day and is now ready to go out.

Something that is taking place at this moment:

He has been sitting here for two hours.

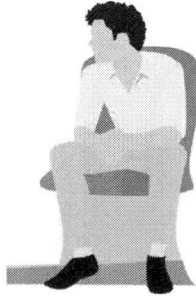

Event in the present can be a habitual event:

I have been living in this house for 30 years.

How to form "Present Perfect progressive" Sentence

The present perfect continuous is formed using the construction

Subject + has/have been + verb (root + -ing) + rest of the sentence

Subject	have/has +been	Verb (V3-ing form)	Rest of sentence
I	have been	living	here for 10 years.
We	have been	playing	football since 8 a.m. morning.
You	have been	practicing	piano for a month now.
He	has been	watching	cartoon movies since childhood.
Jack	has been	reading	this book since January.
They	have been	participating	in flute competition for 5 years.

How to form Present Perfect Progressive "negative sentence"

The present perfect continuous negative is formed using the construction hasn't/haven't been + the present participle (root + -ing).

Below is the structure

Subject+ has/have +not+ been+ verb (v3) + rest of the sentence

Subject	have/has + not+ been	Verb(V3) Pre. participle	Rest of sentence
I	haven't been	living	here for 10 years.
We	haven't been	waiting	for the train all day.
You	haven't been	practicing	the piano for a month now.
Jim	hasn't been	watching	the cartoon movie since childhood.
They	haven't	participating	in guitar

	been		competition for five years.

How to form Present Perfect progressive "Question sentence"

To create a Present Perfect progressive question sentence ,start the question with Have or Has, (Haven't or Hasn't for a negative question) then add a subject (the person or thing that has been doing the action) followed by been and the ing (present participle) form of the verb and only then add the rest of the sentence.

Have/Has+ subject+ been+ verb v3+ rest of the sentence?

Aux Verb have/has	Subject	Been +Verb (Present Participle)	Rest of sentence
Have	I	been working	since 8 a.m. morning?
Have	we	been helping	our team to deliver the project?

Have	you	been living	here for 10 years?
Has	he	been reading	this book all day?
Have	they	been playing	football since last year?

Present Perfect Simple or Present Perfect Progressive (Continuous) – Which one to use?

Both tenses are used to express an action began in the past and is still going on or has just finished. In many cases, both forms are correct, but there is often a difference in meaning: We use the *Present Perfect Simple* mainly to express that an action is completed or to emphasize the result. We use the *Present Perfect Progressive* to emphasize the duration or continuous course of an action.

This difference is often used to talk about different kinds of results in the present. The present perfect simple is used when the action is finished, and the result comes from the action being finished:

She has done all her homework, so she can relax this evening.

The present perfect continuous is used when the result comes from the action itself. It doesn't matter if the whole action is finished or not. The result is often something we can see, hear, smell, or feel:

She has been doing her homework, so she's tired.

Simple Past Tense

The simple past tense of verbs expresses events or actions that already occurred. These actions are finite in that they have both a starting and a stopping point.

Examples of the simple past tense

Action in the past taking place once, never or several times

My grandparents visited us every Sunday.

Actions in the past taking place one after the other

My mother came in, cooked food and served dinner.

Action in the past taking place in the middle of another action

Example: When we were having dinner, the phone suddenly rang.

If sentences type II (If I studied, ...)

Example: If I studied well, I would score good marks in Exams.

As described above there are four types of Past Tense

1. Past Simple

2. Past Continuous or Past Progressive

3. Past Perfect

4. Past Perfect Continuous or Past Perfect Progressive

How to form "Simple past" Sentence

The past simple is usually formed by adding d, ed, or ied to the base form of the verb, however, in English there are many irregular verbs that take on a completely different form in the past tense.

Subject+ main verb(v2) + rest of the sentence

Subject	Verb	rest of sentence
I	went	to my friend's house.
We	liked	that movie.
You	helped	me to study.
He	played	well.
They	liked	my speech.

How to form Simple Past "negative sentence"

When creating negative sentences, we usually use the auxiliary verbs did not + the base form of the verb. You can also use the contraction didn't instead of did not.

Subject+ did+ not + main verb(v1) + rest of the sentence

Subject	axillary verb	Verb	rest of sentence
I	didn't	go	to play.
We	didn't	like	that movie.
You	didn't	tell	me the truth.
She	didn't	dance	well.
They	didn't	know	how to play this game.

How to form Simple Past "Question sentence"

To create a question, start the question with Did, then add a subject (the person or thing that does the action) followed by the base form of the verb and then add the rest of the sentence.

Did+ Subject+ main verb(v1) + rest of the sentence?

Aux verb	Subject	Verb	rest of sentence
Did	I	buy	the right book?
Did	we	play	football?
Did	you	eat	pizza?
Did	he	watch	movie?
Did	they	dance	well?

How to form Simple Past negative question sentence

To create a question, start the question with Did, then add a subject (the person or thing that does the action) followed by the base form of the verb and then add the rest of the sentence.

Did+ Subject+ not+ main verb(v1) + rest of the sentence?

Aux. verb	Subject	not	Verb	rest of sentence
Did	I	not	buy	the right book?

Did	we	not	play	football?
Did	you	not	eat	pizza?
Did	he	not	watch	TV?
Did	they	not	dance	well?

Past- Progressive

It is also named as Past Continuous. The past continuous describes actions or events which began in the past and is still going on at the time of speaking. In other words, it expresses an unfinished or incomplete action in the past.

The past continuous/progressive is used in several instances:

For something which continued before and after another action:

As I was watching television the phone rang.

Refer to a habitual action in the past.

I was practicing guitar every day .

To show that something continued for some time:

Everyone was playing in the ground.

With verbs which show change or growth:

The vegetables were growing up quickly.

How to form "Past Progressive" Sentence

This is the structure to form a past progressive sentence.

Subject +auxiliary verb (was/were) + main verb (present participle) + Rest of the Sentence

Subject	Aux. verb	Main Verb (Present Participle/ing form)	Rest of sentence
I	was	writing	a book.
We	were	eating	lunch at three o'clock.

You	were	playing	football.
She	was	solving	the crossword puzzles.
They	were	watching	movie.

How to form Past Progressive "negative sentence"

This is the structure to form a past progressive negative sentence.

Subject +auxiliary verb (was/were) + not + main verb (present participle)+ Rest of the Sentence

Note :

When shortening a form of be and negative, just remove the o in not and add an apostrophe (')

was not > wasn't

were not > weren't

Subject	Aux. verb	not	Verb (ing form)	Rest of sentence

I	was	not	eating	my lunch.
We	were	not	hiking	that mountain.
You	were	not	playing	Baseball.
She	was	not	feeling	well.
They	were	not	watching	TV.

How to form Past Progressive "Question sentence"

This is the structure to form a past progressive question sentence.

Auxiliary verb (was/were) + Subject + main verb (present participle)+ Rest of the Sentence ?

Aux. verb (was/were)	Subject	main verb (present participle)	Rest of sentence
Was	I	talking	too much?
Were	we	buying	Pizza for lunch?

Were	you	playing	Football?
Was	he	watching	TV?
Were	they	riding	their bikes.

How to form Past Progressive "Interrogative negative sentence"

This is the structure to form a past progressive Interrogative negative sentence.

Auxiliary Verb (was/were)+ Subject+ not+ main verb (present participle) + rest of the sentence?

Aux. verb	Subject	not	Verb	rest of sentence
Was	I	not	playing	baseball?
Were	you	not	eating	pizza?
Was	he	not	watching	TV?
Were	they	not	going	there?

<u>Past Perfect Tense</u>

The past perfect tense is used to describe one action that happened before another action in the past. It is used to make it clear that one event happened before another in the past.

The past perfect is used in several instances:

To show that an action happened before something else in the past:

I couldn't get into the house. I had lost my keys.

In reported speech:

-The past perfect is common when we report people's words or thoughts.

Jack said that he had never tasted pizza before.

In if (conditional) sentences:

The past perfect tense is used in unreal or hypothetical situations, as in the following sentences:

I would have helped him if he had asked.

For something we had done several times up to a point in the past and continued to do after that point:

He had written three books and he was working on another one.

How to form "Past Perfect" Sentence

In order to form a sentence in the past perfect, choose a subject the person or thing that has done the action, add an auxiliary (or helping) verb: had + the past participle form of the verb and then add the rest of the sentence.

This is the structure to form a past perfect sentence.

Subject+ auxiliary verb (had)+ main verb (past participle) + rest of the sentence

Subject	had+verb(v3)	Rest of sentence
I	had played	basketball.
We	had waited	for the train.

You	had met	him before.
Jack	had kept	my books.
He	had lived	here for 5 years.
They	had eaten	their lunch.

How to form Past Perfect "negative sentence"

This is the structure to form a past perfect negative sentence.

Subject+ auxiliary verb(had) + not + main verb (past participle) + rest of the sentence

Subject	Aux. verb (had)	not	Verb(V3) Past participle	Rest of sentence
I	had	not	played	basketball.
We	had	not	gone	to Paris.
You	had	not	met	him before.
He	had	not	kept	my books.

Jack	had	not	lived	here.
They	had	not	eaten	their lunch.

How to form Past Perfect "Interrogative sentence"

This is the structure to form a past perfect Interrogative sentence.

Auxiliary verb(had) + Subject + main verb (past participle) + rest of the sentence?

Aux. Verb/ had	Subject	Verb in V3 (Past Participle)	Rest of sentence
Had	I	eaten	more cake?
Had	we	begun	the meeting yet?
Had	you	gone	to Paris before?
Had	he	gone	to school today?
Had	they	ridden	their new bikes?

How to form Past Perfect "Negative Interrogative sentence"

This is the structure to form a past perfect negative Interrogative sentence.

Auxiliary Verb (had) + Subject+ not+ main verb (past participle) + rest of the sentence?

Axillary verb /had	Subject	not	Verb	rest of sentence
Had	I	not	eaten	my lunch?
Had	you	not	gone	to school?
Had	he	not	watched	TV?
Had	they	not	gone	to play?

Past- Perfect Progressive

The past perfect progressive (also called past perfect continuous) is a verb tense which is used to show that an action started in the past and continued up to another point in the past.

The past perfect progressive is used in several instances:

An action that started and ended before a certain time in the past, but the effect of this action was still important at that moment

Example:

When I met John, he was tired because he had been playing all day.

An action that started before a certain time in the past and wasn't completed at that time

Example:

Jack had been practicing music for a very long time, but he still hadn't achieved any award.

An action that started before a certain time in the past and was interrupted by a second action

Example:

John had been studying for hours when mom knocked on the door.

How to form "Past Perfect progressive" Sentence

The past perfect continuous is formed using the construction

Subject + had been + verb present participle (root + -ing) + rest of the sentence

Subject	had been	Verb(V3) Present participle	Rest of sentence
I	had been	sleeping	for 9 hours.
We	have been	waiting	for the train for 2 hours when it arrived.
You	had been	practicing	since 8 a.m. morning.
He	had been	watching	the cartoon movie since childhood.
They	had been	living	here for 10 yrs.

How to form Past Perfect Progressive "negative sentence"

The past perfect continuous negative is formed using the construction had not been + the present participle (root + -ing).

Below is the structure

Subject+ had +not+ been+ verb (v3) + rest of the sentence

Subject	had + not + been	Verb(V3) Past participle	Rest of sentence
I	had not been	living	here for 10 years.
We	had not been	waiting	for the train all day.
You	had not been	practicing	the piano for a month now.
Jim	had not been	watching	the cartoon movie since childhood.
They	had not been	playing	basketball since morning.

How to form Past Perfect progressive "Question sentence"

Below is the structure to form past perfect progressive sentence.

Had + subject+ been+ verb v3+ rest of the sentence?

Aux. verb /had	Subject	Been +Verb in V3 (Past Participle)	Rest of sentence
Had	I	been working	since Monday?
Had	we	been waiting	for you since 5 hrs.?
Had	you	been living	here for 30 years?
Had	he	been sleeping	for 3 hrs.?
Had	they	been playing	baseball since 8 a.m. morning?

Future Tense

As described above there are four types of Future Tense

1. Future Simple or Future Indefinite

2. Future Continuous or Future Progressive

3. Future Perfect

4. Future Perfect Continuous or Future Perfect Progressive

Time expressions in the Future Tense

There are several time expressions that are used in all of the different forms of the future tense. They are generally used at the end of the sentence or question. The most common are: tomorrow, next week (month/year), in two days (weeks, months years), the day after tomorrow.

Future Simple

It is also named as Future Indefinite Tense. The simple future tense is used to describe an action that will take place in future.

Examples of the simple future tense

Here are some example sentences showing different ways that we can use the simple future tense:

To predict a future event:

It will snow tomorrow.

Describe a simple action in the future:

My grandparents will come to our house next week.

To express willingness:

I will help to carry your luggage.

How to form "Future Simple" Sentence

This is the structure to form a future simple or future indefinite sentence.

Subject+ Auxiliary verb(will/shall)+Main verb(1st form) + Rest of the Sentence

Subject	Auxiliary verb(will/shall)	Verb	rest of sentence
I	shall/will	go	home tomorrow.
We	will	play	basketball.

You	will	learn	a new language.
He/She/Jack	will	watch	a cartoon movie.
They	will	live	in New York.

How to form Simple Future "negative sentence"

When creating negative sentences, we usually use the auxiliary verbs will not + the base form of the verb. You can also use the contraction won't instead of will not.

This is the structure to form a future simple negative sentence.

Subject+ will not + verb+ rest of the Sentence

Subject	Aux verb (will) + not	Verb	Rest of sentence
I	won't	go	to school tomorrow.
We	won't	watch	movie tonight.

You	won't	come	to dance.
He	won't	solve	crossword puzzles.
They	won't	come	to New York.

How to form Simple Future "Interrogative sentence"

To create a question that will be answered with a yes or no, use Will/Shall + subject + base form of the verb.

This is the structure to form a future simple Interrogative sentence.

Auxiliary Verb (Will/Shall) + Subject+ Verb+ Rest of the Sentence?

Axillary verb	Subject	Verb	rest of sentence
Will/Shall	I	ride	your bike?
Will	you	join	us?
Will	he	dance	on stage?
Will	they	come	to play with us?

How to form Simple Future "Interrogative negative sentence"

This is the structure to form a future simple Interrogative negative sentence.

Auxiliary Verb (Will/Shall) + Subject+ not+ Verb(1st form)+ Rest of the Sentence?

Axillary verb	Subject	not	Verb	rest of sentence
Will/Shall	I	not	work	on it?
Will	you	not	take	the exam?
Will	he	not	do	it?
Will	they	not	go	to play?

Future- Progressive

It is also named as Future Continuous. The future progressive tense is used for an on-going action that will occur in the future.

The future continuous/progressive is used in several instances:

To say that something will be in progress at a particular moment in the future:

This time tomorrow I will be playing tennis with my friends.

For predicting or guessing about future events:

I guess, John will be coming to the meeting.

Used to make polite enquiries about people's plans:

We are going out to play, will you be coming with us ?

How to form "Future Progressive" Sentence

This is the structure to form a future progressive or future continuous sentence.

Subject+ Auxiliary verb(will be/shall be)+Main verb(ing form) + Rest of the Sentence

Subject	Aux. verb(will be /shall be)	Verb	rest of sentence

I	shall be/will be	going	to beach next week.
We	will be	playing	basketball.
You	will be	learning	a new language.
He/She/Jack	will be	coming	to support our team.
They	will be	living	in New York.

How to form "Future Progressive" negative Sentence

This is the structure to form a future progressive or future continuous negative sentence.

Subject + Auxiliary verb (will /shall) + not + be+ main verb(ing form) + Rest of the Sentence

Subject	Auxiliary verb(will /shall)+ not+ be	Verb	rest of sentence
I	shall not be/will not be	going	to beach next week.

We	will not be	playing	basketball.
You	will not be	learning	a new language.
He/She/Jack	will not be	coming	to support our team.
They	will not be	living	in New York.

How to form Future progressive "Interrogative sentence"

This is the structure to form a future progressive Interrogative sentence.

Auxiliary Verb (Will/Shall) + Subject+ be+ main verb(Ing form)+ Rest of the Sentence?

Aux. verb	Subject	be	Verb(ing form)	rest of sentence
Will/Shall	I	be	riding	your bike?
Will	you	be	coming	with us?
Will	he	be	going	to the birthday party?

Will	they	be	eating	pizza for dinner?

How to form Future progressive "Interrogative negative sentence"

This is the structure to form a future progressive Interrogative negative sentence.

Auxiliary Verb (Will/Shall) + Subject + not +be + Verb(ing form)+ Rest of the Sentence?

Aux. verb	Subject	not	be	Verb	rest of sentence
Will/Shall	I	not	be	going	there?
Will	you	not	be	taking	the exam?
Will	he	not	be	coming	with us?
Will	they	not	be	eating	pizza for dinner?

Future Perfect

Future perfect tense refers to a completed action in the future. When we use this tense, we are projecting ourselves forward into the future and looking back at an action that will be completed sometime later than now. It is most often used with a time expression.

How to form "Future Perfect" Sentence

This is the structure to form a future perfect sentence.

Subject+ Auxiliary verb(will have /shall have)+Main verb(past participle form) + Rest of the Sentence

Subject	Aux. verb(will have /shall have)	Main Verb(V3)	rest of sentence
I	shall have/will have	taken	my breakfast.
We	will have	played	basketball.

You	will have	learned	a new language.
He/She/Jac k	will have	complete d	the project report by Monday.
They	will have	taken	admission .

How to form "Future Perfect" negative Sentence

This is the structure to form a future perfect negative sentence.

Subject + Auxiliary verb(will /shall) + not + have + main verb(past participle form) + Rest of the Sentence

Subject	Auxiliary verb(will /shall)+ not+ have	Verb	rest of sentence
I	shall not have/will not have	taken	my breakfast.
We	will not have	come	to play with you.

You	will not have	learned	a new language.
He/She/Jack	will not have	joined	our team.
They	will not have	lived	in New York.

How to form Future perfect "Interrogative sentence"

This is the structure to form a future perfect Interrogative sentence.

Auxiliary Verb (Will/Shall) + Subject+ have+ verb (past participle form)+ Rest of the Sentence?

Axillary verb	Subject	have	Verb(v3 form)	rest of sentence
Will/Shall	I	have	written	neatly?
Will	you	have	started	your journey?
Will	he	have	gone	to the birthday party?
Will	they	have	eaten	Pizza for dinner?

How to form Future perfect "Interrogative negative sentence"

This is the structure to form a future perfect Interrogative negative sentence.

Auxiliary Verb (Will/Shall) + Subject + not + have + Verb (past participle form) + Rest of the Sentence?

Aux. verb	Subject	not	have	Verb	rest of sentence
Will/Shall	I	not	have	worked	on it?
Will	you	not	have	taken	the exam?
Will	he	not	have	come	with us?
Will	they	not	have	eaten	pizza for dinner?

Future Perfect Progressive

This tense is used to describe an ongoing action that will complete in future. It is used to express the ongoing nature of an action with regards to its continuation towards a point in future. The action is assumed to be continued for a time (specified or unspecified) in future. A 'time-reference' is used in the sentence to show starting time of the action or for how long the action continues.

How to form "Future Perfect progressive" Sentence

This is the structure to form a future perfect progressive sentence.

Subject+ Auxiliary verb(will have been/shall have been)+Main verb(ing form) + Rest of the Sentence

Subject	Aux. verb(will have /shall have)	Main Verb(V3)	rest of sentence
I	shall have been/will have been	studying	for two hours.
We	will have been	playing	basketball since morning.
You	will have been	learning	a new language for two months.

He/She/Jack	will have been	reading	this book since morning.
They	will have been	living	in New York for 5 yrs.

How to form "Future Perfect progressive" negative Sentence

This is the structure to form a future perfect progressive negative sentence.

Subject + Auxiliary verb(will /shall) + not + have been+ main verb(ing form) + Rest of the Sentence

Subject	Auxiliary verb (will /shall) + not	have been	Verb(ing form)	rest of sentence
I	shall not /will not	have been	studying	for two hours.
We	will not	have been	playing	games since March.
You	will not	have been	using	Your bike since December.

He/She/Jack	will not	have been	living	here for 5 years.
They	will not	have been	working	since morning.

How to form Future perfect progressive "Interrogative sentence"

This is the structure to form a future perfect progressive Interrogative sentence.

Auxiliary Verb (Will/Shall) + Subject+ have been+ verb(ing form form) + Rest of the Sentence?

Aux. verb	Subject	Have been	Verb (ing form)	rest of sentence
Will/Shall	I	have been	eating	vegetables for three months?
Will	you	have been	working	in this project since June?
Will	he	have been	reading	since morning?
Will	they	have been	making	noise for two hours?

How to form Future perfect progressive "Interrogative negative sentence"

This is the structure to form a future perfect progressive Interrogative negative sentence.

Auxiliary Verb (Will/Shall) + Subject + not + have been+ Verb(past participle form)+ Rest of the Sentence?

Aux. verb	Subject	not	have been	Verb (ing form)	rest of sentence
Will/Shall	I	not	have been	working	here for 2 year?
Will	you	not	have been	waiting	for the result since Monday?
Will	he	not	have been	studying	here for two years?
Will	they	not	have been	making	noise since last night?

A time-reference is used in the sentence to show starting time of the action or for how long the action continues. For time-reference of the action, two specific words 'since' and 'for' are used in the sentence.

Since is used if the exact starting time (since Monday, since 8 A.M, etc.) of the action is known or intended to be shown in the sentence.

For is used to express the amount of time (e.g. for 10 hours, for 4 months, for two years) for which the action continued towards a point in future.

■■■

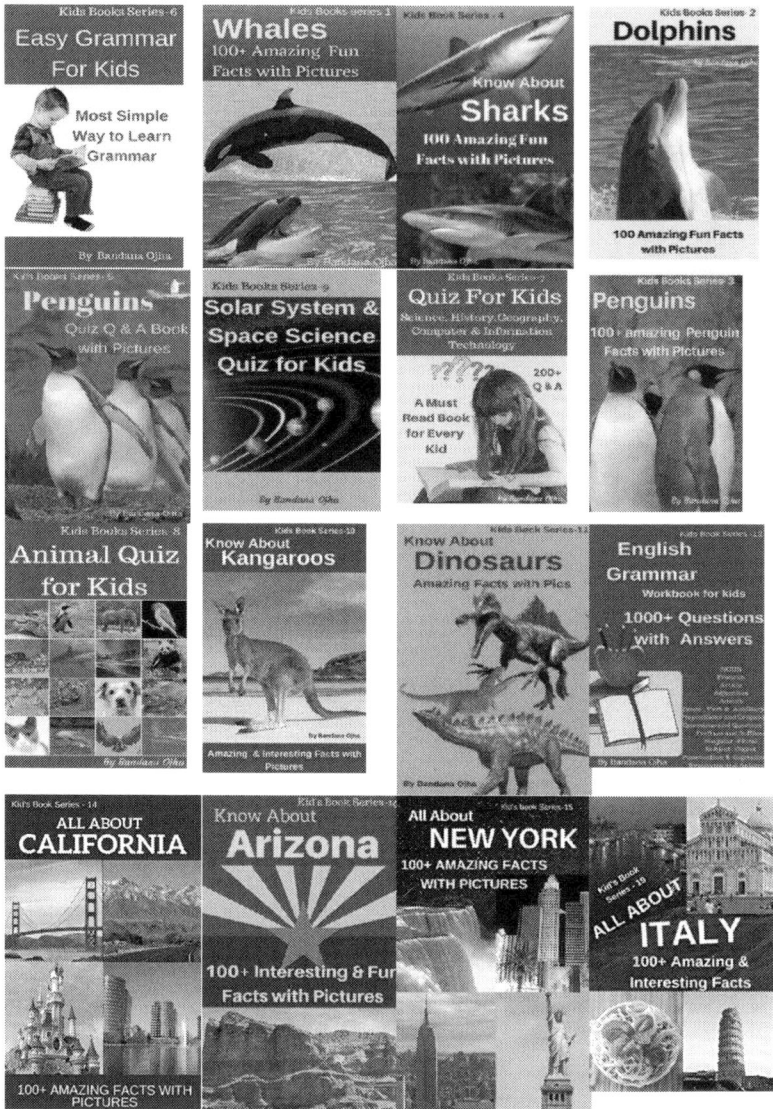

Kids Books Series-6
Easy Grammar For Kids
Most Simple Way to Learn Grammar
By Bandana Ojha

Kids Books series 1
Whales
100+ Amazing Fun Facts with Pictures

Kids Book Series - 4
Know About
Sharks
100 Amazing Fun Facts with Pictures

Kids Books Series- 2
Dolphins
100 Amazing Fun Facts with Pictures

Penguins
Quiz Q & A Book with Pictures

Kids Books Series -9
Solar System & Space Science Quiz for Kids
By Bandana Ojha

Quiz For Kids
Science, History, Geography, Computer & Information Technology
200+ Q & A
A Must Read Book for Every Kid

Kids Books Series 3
Penguins
100+ amazing Penguin Facts with Pictures
By Bandana Ojha

Kids Books Series- 8
Animal Quiz for Kids
By Bandana Ojha

Kids Book Series-10
Know About
Kangaroos
By Bandana Ojha
Amazing & Interesting Facts with Pictures

Kids Book Series-11
Know About
Dinosaurs
Amazing Facts with Pics
By Bandana Ojha

Kids Book Series -13
English Grammar
Workbook for kids
1000+ Questions with Answers

Kid's Book Series - 14
ALL ABOUT
CALIFORNIA
100+ AMAZING FACTS WITH PICTURES

Kid's Book Series-19
Know About
Arizona
100+ Interesting & Fun Facts with Pictures

All About
NEW YORK
100+ AMAZING FACTS WITH PICTURES

Kid's book Series-15
Kid's Book Series - 16
ALL ABOUT
ITALY
100+ Amazing & Interesting Facts

Printed in Great Britain
by Amazon